DOTS & SPOTS

A SUPER-DUPER SQUIGGLY DOODLE & DRAWING BOOK

Brimming with creative inspiration, how-to projects, and useful information to enrich your everyday life, Quarto Knows is a favorite destination for those pursuing their interests and passions. Visit our site and dig deeper with our books into your area of interest: Quarto Creates, Quarto Cooks, Quarto Homes, Quarto Lives, Quarto Drives, Quarto Explores, Quarto Gifts, or Quarto Kids.

© 2020 Quarto Publishing Group USA Inc.
Text and illustrations © 2020 Kelli Chipponeri & Ryan Hayes

First published in 2020 by Walter Foster Jr., an imprint of The Quarto Group.
26391 Crown Valley Parkway, Suite 220, Mission Viejo, CA 92691, USA.
T (949) 380-7510 F (949) 380-7575 **www.QuartoKnows.com**

Walter Foster Jr. titles are also available at discount for retail, wholesale, promotional, and bulk purchase. For details, contact the Special Sales Manager by email at specialsales@quarto.com or by mail at The Quarto Group, Attn: Special Sales Manager, 100 Cummings Center, Suite 265D, Beverly, MA 01915, USA.

ISBN: 978-1-63322-894-8

Digital edition published in 2020
eISBN: 978-1-63322-895-5

Printed in China
10 9 8 7 6 5 4 3 2

DOTS & SPOTS

A SUPER-DUPER SQUIGGLY DOODLE & DRAWING BOOK

KELLI CHIPPONERI &
RYAN HAYES

HOW TO USE THIS BOOK

Each page of this book includes drawing prompts, circles, ovals, dots, and spots of different sizes waiting for you to fill them in! The only things you need are your imagination and a pencil to create exciting, and sometimes silly, pieces of art. Sketch, squiggle, draw, design, doodle, and color to complete these wacky prompts, while finding inspiration in this book and in the world around you!

Grab your favorite drawing tools: pencils, pens, crayons, markers, paints, or stamps.

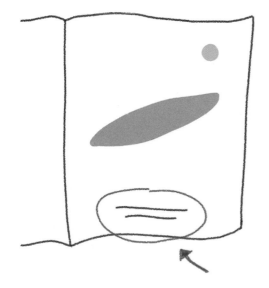

Flip to any spot in this book.

Read the prompt on that page to see what to draw.

Use your imagination and creativity to sketch, squiggle, draw, design, doodle, and color hilarious and quirky art!

What's going on here?
Lots of circles, big and
small, short and tall!
Use the circles to create
silly faces of real and
imaginary animals.

What can these spots be? Maybe it's you on the back of a super-friendly dragon or an out-of-this-world flying saucer? It can be anything you want, so draw it in!

Draw what you see here. Could this be a lake filled
with grape juice or bears on roller skates?

This bag is filled with magical tokens that grant 300 wishes!
Draw the bag above and what you would wish for on the next page.

Doodle a monster using this spot.
How many eyes does it have?
Does it have horns or a big nose?
What color is its fur or scales?

Design time! What time is it? Draw a clock or watch.
Is it hanging on a wall, sitting on a table,
or strapped to your wrist?

This is the planet Yak.
Do you think aliens live here? Draw them.

Is that hot cocoa exploding out of that volcano?
Draw a mug so you can drink some!
Add marshmallows or whipped cream.

Watch out for those flying donuts! Decorate them with frosting and sprinkles. Add some jelly in the middle if you'd like. Yum!

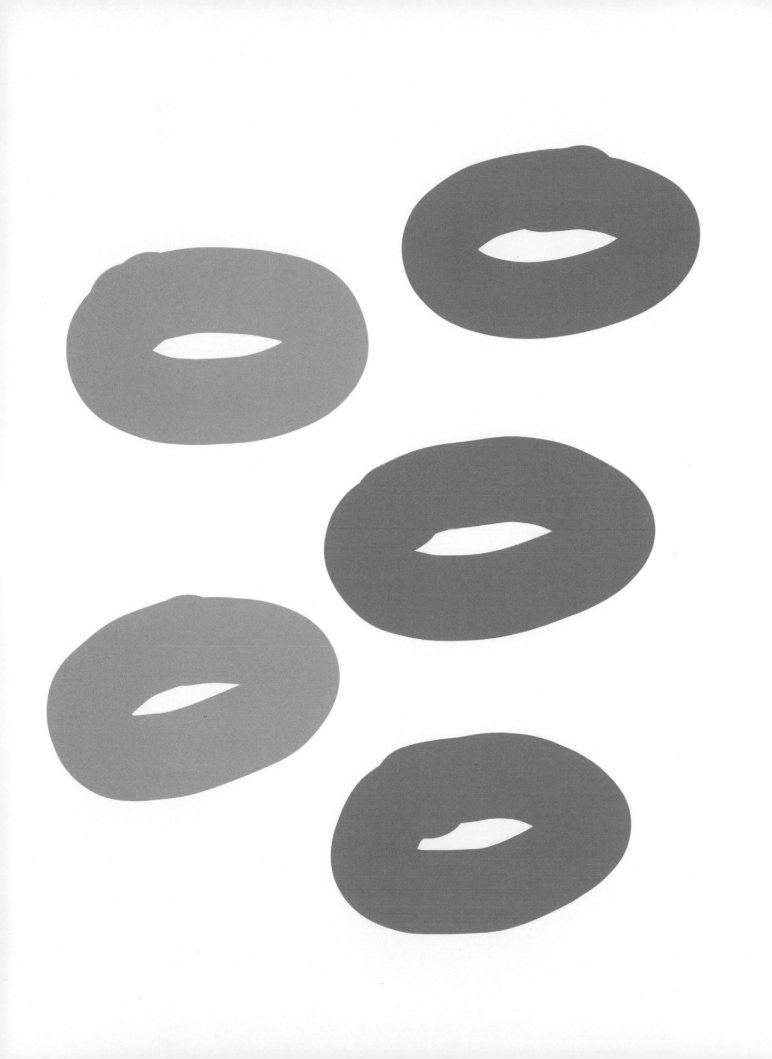

Mirror, mirror on the wall...who's the fairest of them all?
It's you! Draw yourself here!

Now draw yourself in a fun house mirror!

Help this robot do the robot dance by
drawing its head, body, arms, and legs.

Draw a robot friend. What do you think
two robots would say to each other?

Draw round things on each of these circles. Some ideas include balls, clocks, and planets. What other things can you think of that are round?

Cool! It's a vehicle from the future.
Does it have tires, doors, or wings?

It's your best friend's birthday, so decorate a cake!
Don't forget to write their name on top and add
the correct number of candles!

These are the spots of a colorful cow jumping over the moon!
Draw the cow around the spots.

Oh no! The dish is running away with the spoon!
Draw the dish a face, arms, and legs.

Welcome to Ocean Beach. Here's your beach ball, but did you bring an umbrella, a towel, and a picnic lunch?

Draw everything you brought to
complete this beach scene.

Look! Meatballs! Draw the spaghetti underneath
and the person eating this delicious dish!
Are they using a fork, a spoon, or chopsticks?

Build an ice cream cone or sundae with a cherry on top!

Who is playing this bean bag toss game?

Is it a dinosaur family or a herd of horses?
Are they wearing matching hats or shirts?

Can you see these polar bears fishing through a hole in the ice?
Have they caught a catfish, dog-fish, or bird-fish? Brrr!!!

What mythical creature lives in this undersea cave?
Is it a mermaid or a monster? Create your own sea creature!

These are gumdrops flying toward a candy castle.
Are the castle walls made of taffy and the moat
filled with syrup? Are there cake pops as turrets
and a boat made of waffles? Create a sweet and
sugary palace fit for candy royalty.

What will you have for breakfast today?
Draw your favorite cereal in this bowl.
What **do** you want to drink?

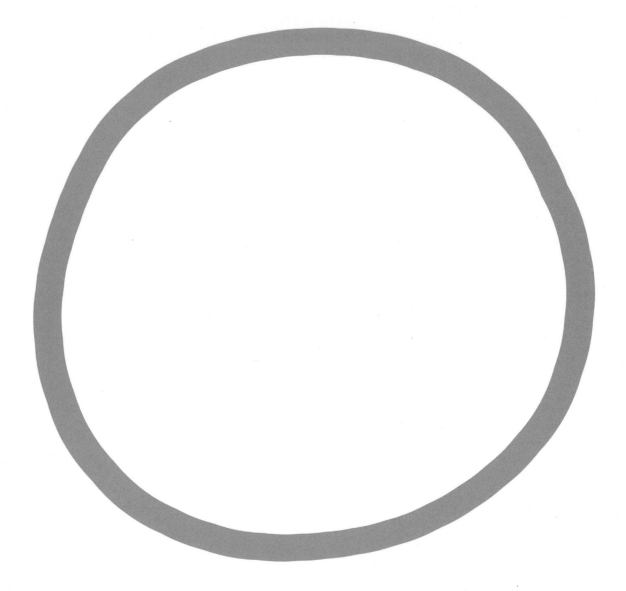

Doodle the arms, legs, and faces on these singing, dancing avocados. Are they wearing shoes, hats, or neckties? What song do you think they're singing?

We all live in a yellow submarine!
Draw the doors, propeller, and periscope
on this underwater vehicle.

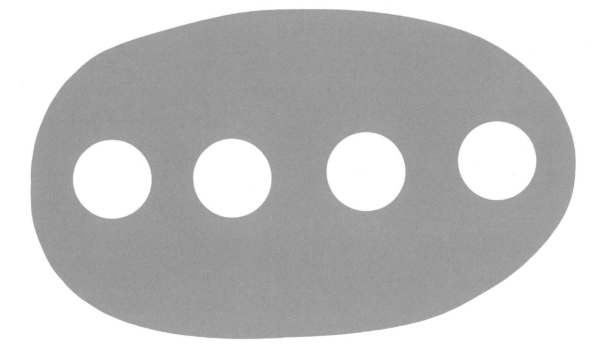

Add some underwater sea life to complete the scene.

The sun is setting on the horizon.
What do you think is happening in this scene?
Use your imagination to draw it here.

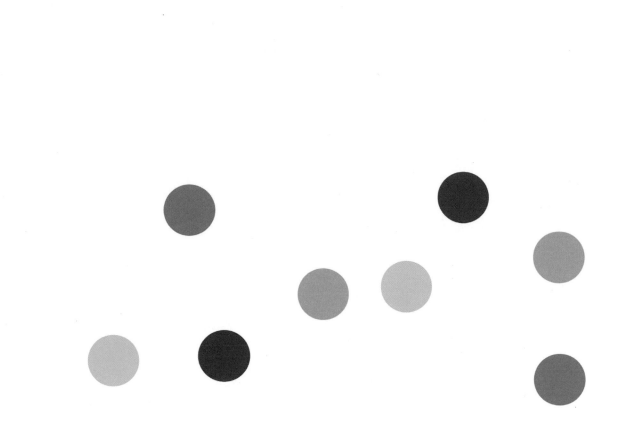

What has eight arms and can juggle?
An octopus! Draw one here juggling all these balls.

Happy birthday to you! Here's a bunch of balloons.
Decorate them with crazy designs.

Oh no! One is flying away.
Can you doodle a long string and catch it?

Look at that spider! Is it standing on a web or hanging from a doorway? Draw its legs! Remember how many it has? Hint: It comes after seven!

Time for tea! Draw a spout, handle, and base
on this teapot. Then draw a cup and saucer
and decorate them with a pattern.

Bullseye! **How many arrows hit the center of this target?**

Is that a giraffe and a kangaroo playing basketball
or soccer? Where is the rest of the team?
Can you draw the whole squad?

Now really stretch your imagination, adding scribbles, squiggles, and anything that makes you giggle! Make faces, patterns, animals, go-carts, fast cars, rocket ships...absolutely anything!

What silly things **do** you see here?

Play ball! Who is here playing baseball? Is that a team of snowmen playing a team of polar bears? Draw each team in their uniforms, including baseball caps and gloves.

This is **Cleo** the **Clown's** nose.
Can you help paint Cleo's face?
Is this clown happy or sad?

Look at this rooftop garden! What's growing here?
Vegetables? Flowers? Herbs?

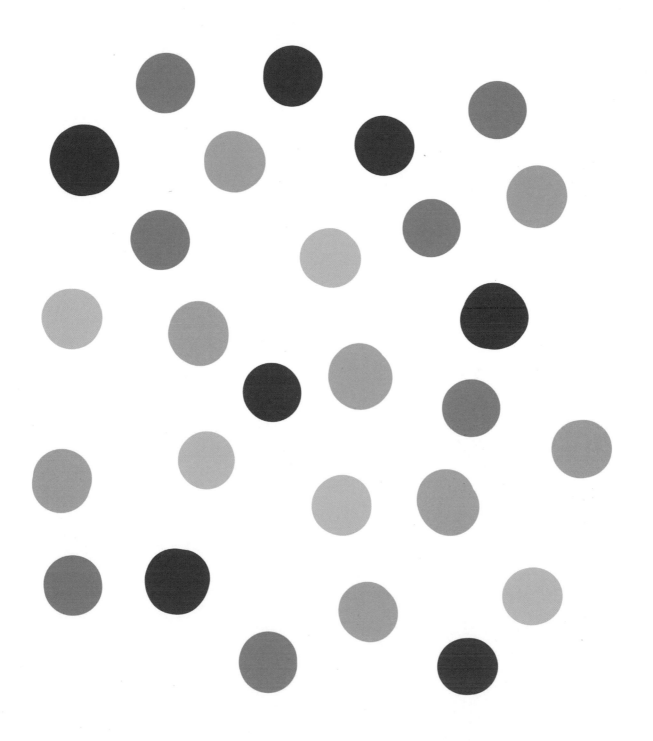

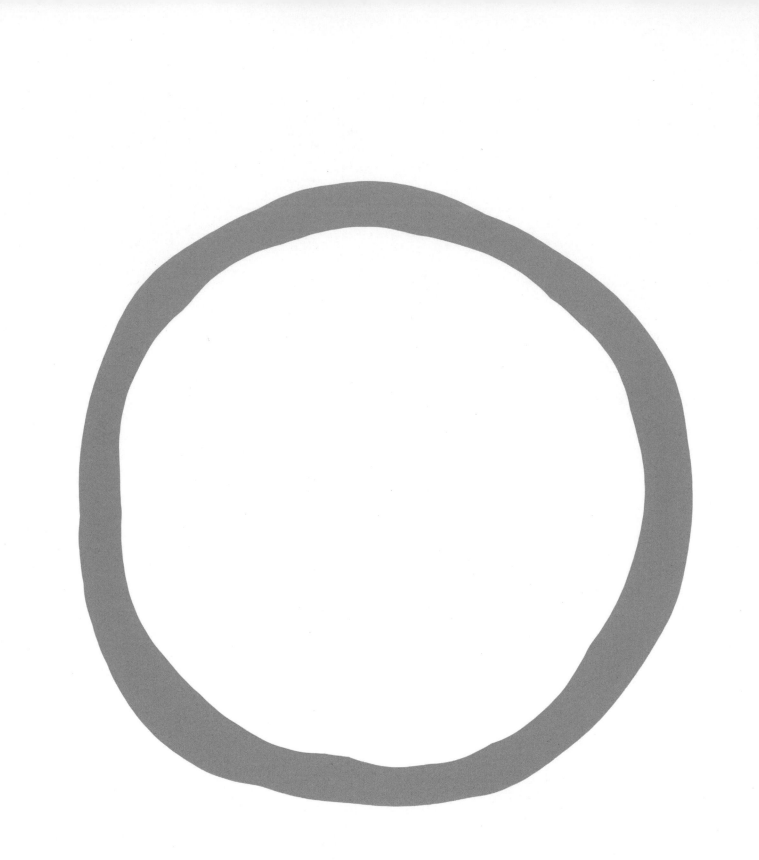

Draw pizzas with pizzazz for you and your friends!

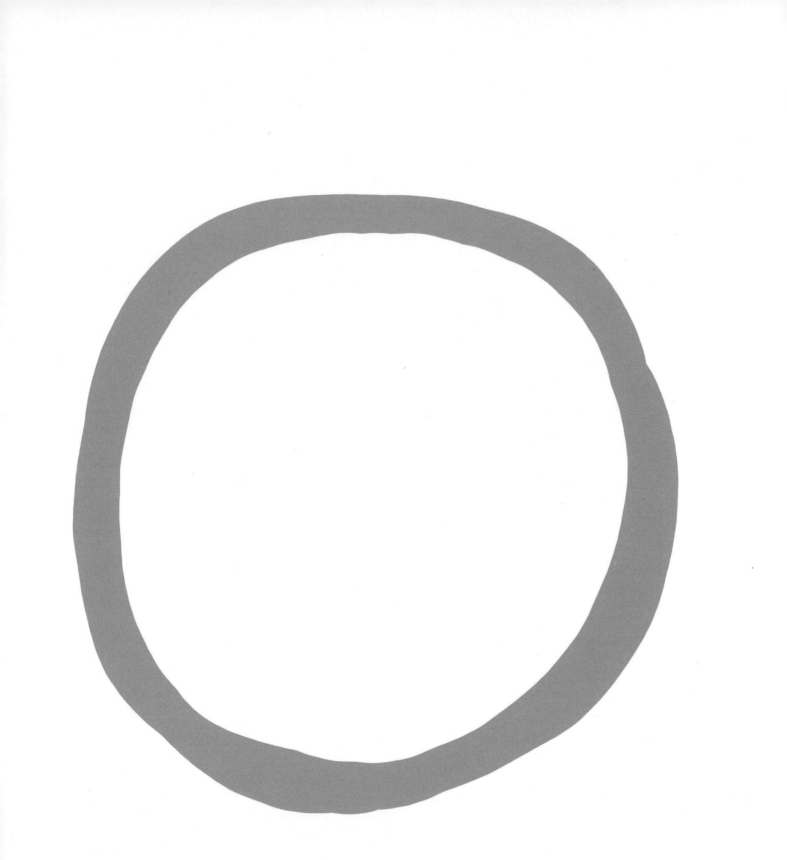

What toppings will you sprinkle on top? Pepperoni, anchovies, candy corn, chocolate chips, or jelly beans?

Trick or treat! Create your own jack-o'-lanterns!

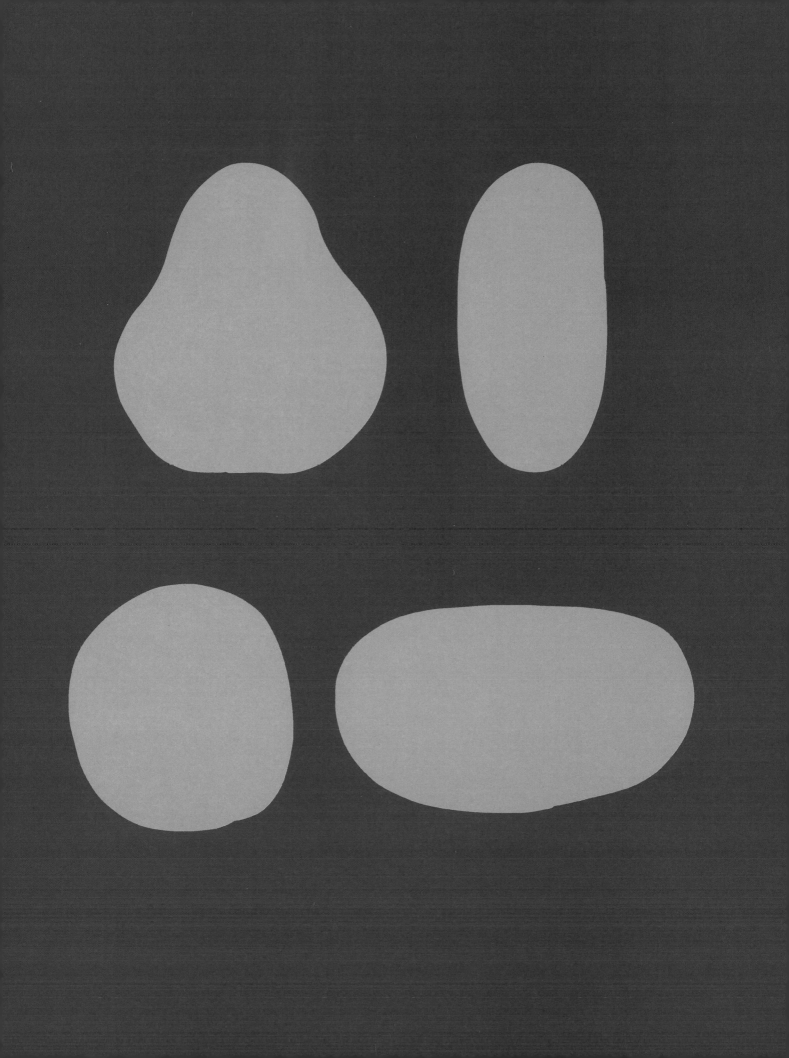

If you could be a superhero, what special powers
would you have? Draw yourself in a superhero
costume holding this shield.

What do you see with those night vision goggles? A hooting owl or an upside-down bat? Maybe it is a Yeti! Draw something you might see only at night.

What is pictured on these coins? Are these coins from
an old treasure chest you found buried in the sand?

Are you, a friend, a family member, or pet
featured on these paper dollar bills?

Welcome to the bowling alley! Draw the person who just
tossed this ball down the lane. Draw in the 10 pins too!
Was it a strike or a gutter ball?

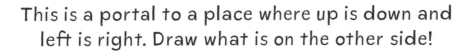

This is a portal to a place where up is down and
left is right. Draw what is on the other side!

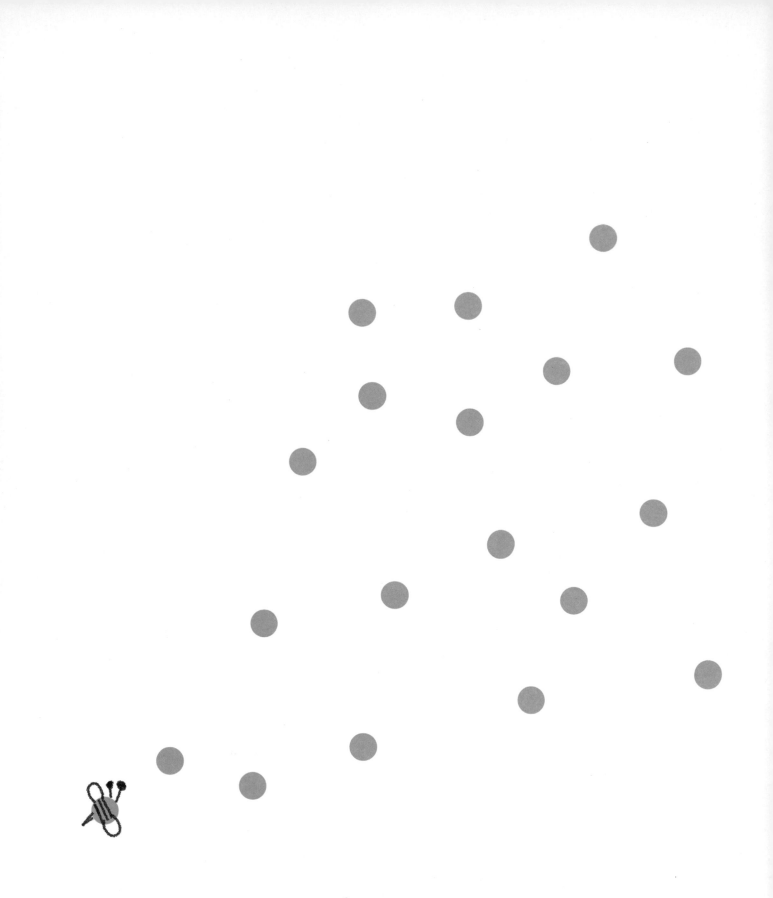

Where is this swarm of bees going? Are they looking for flowers or flying back to their hive?

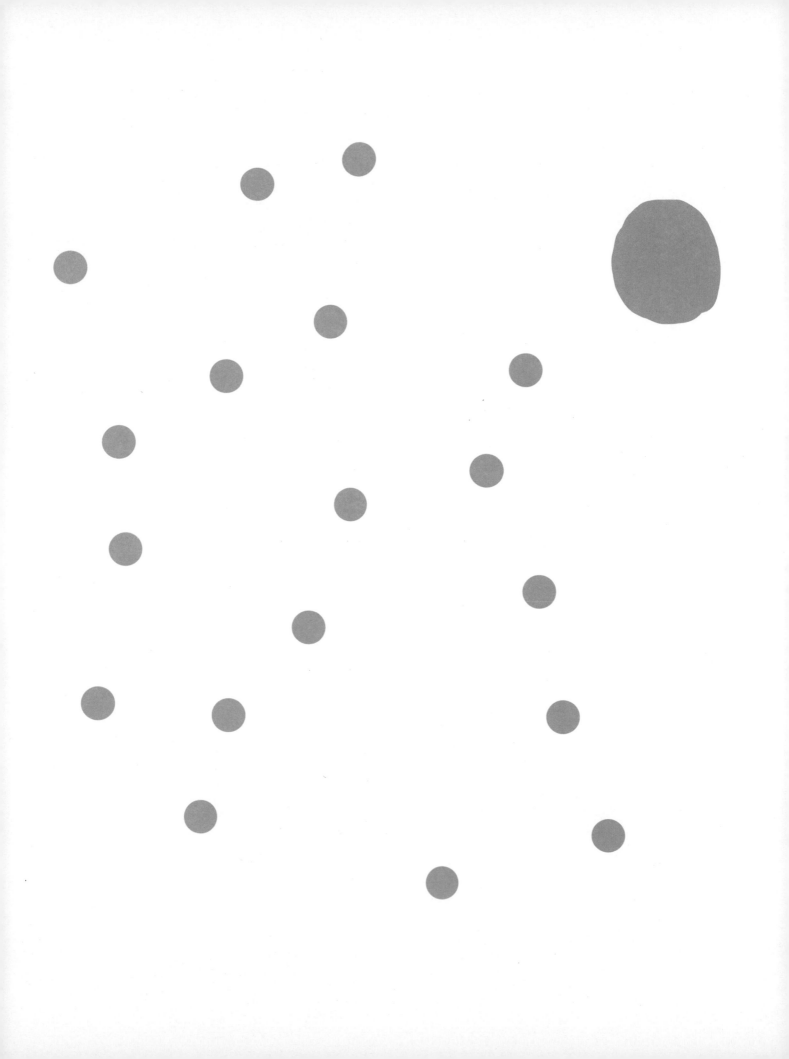

Imagine you have a wall in your closet full of sunglasses.
Design different styles for your different outfits.
Circle your favorite pair!

Imagine you're an alien visiting the planet Earth!
Where would you go first? Draw it here.

What's cooking in that frying pan?
Is it an egg sunny-side up with two pieces of bacon?
Draw your favorite breakfast.

Spin around on this merry-go-round!
Draw all the **different** animals you can ride.

Here's a monster truck jumping off a HUGE ramp.
What does the truck look like?
You decide and draw it here.

Draw who is tossing that Frisbee!

Who will catch it?

Look! You're at a rock concert! Draw someone
playing the drums and someone playing the guitar.

How many more band members are there?
Draw them, too, or the band won't sound so good!

'Tis the season! Decorate your own holiday wreath.
Don't forget to add some ribbon and a bow.

Take a peek in this mouse hole and doodle
what you see inside. Does a mouse family live
here? Are there tiny tables and chairs?

What's on the other side of a black hole?
Silly-dilly aliens in spaceships?
Or super-duper slippery sharks
swimming through space? You decide.

Peer into this magician hat.
What will you pull out?
Is it a bouquet of flowers, a fluffy rabbit,
or something else? Draw the magic!

Who is swimming in this pool? Who is floating in the inner tube? Who is that swinging on the tire swing? SPLASH!

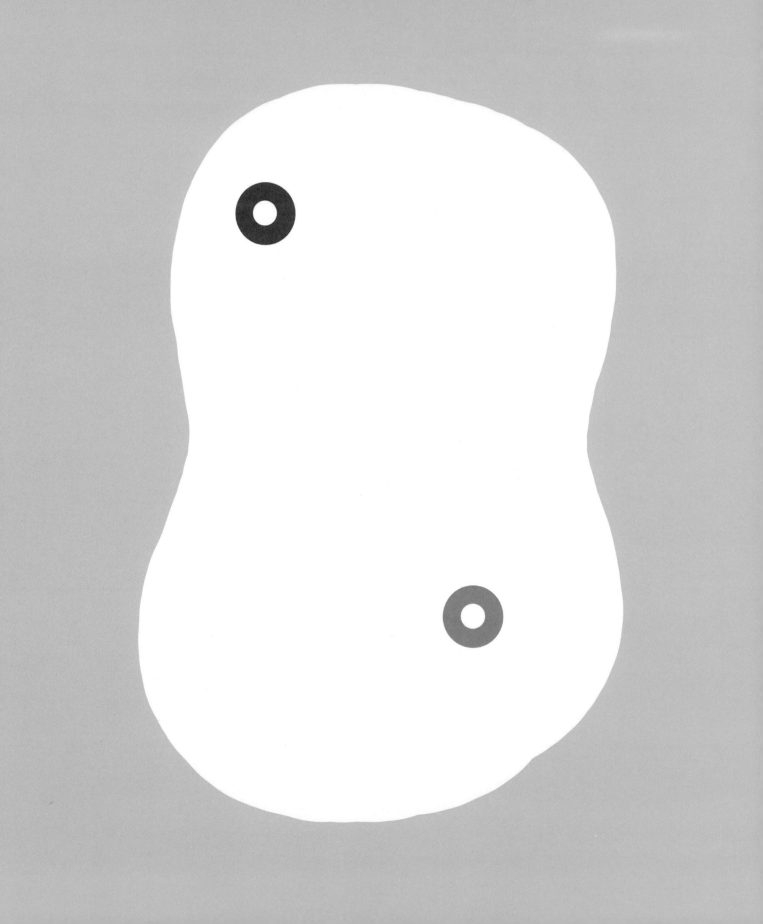

Design your own crazy miniature golf course.
Draw the obstacles in your path
from the golf ball to the hole.

Unicycles! Bicycles! Tricycles!
Doodle a bunch of silly bikes!

Imagine you are a jewelry designer, and these dots and spots are your jewels. Can you design some necklaces, rings, bracelets, and earrings?

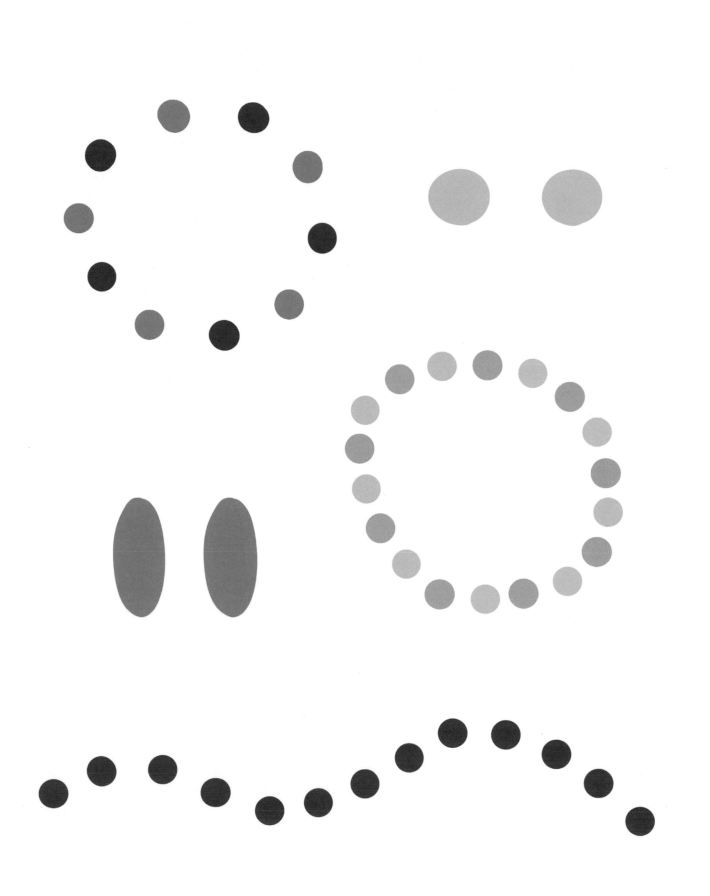

Your spaceship is headed right toward this thing, but what is it? Is it a moon made of cheese where you can make a safe landing?

Design your own mask. Do you want your mask to be crazy, funny, or scary? Is there a smile or a frown? Does it have glasses or an eye patch?

Here is a knot hole in a tree. What would fit inside? A family of squirrels or a bird's nest? Draw who you imagine lives here.

Holy moley, that's lots of spots!

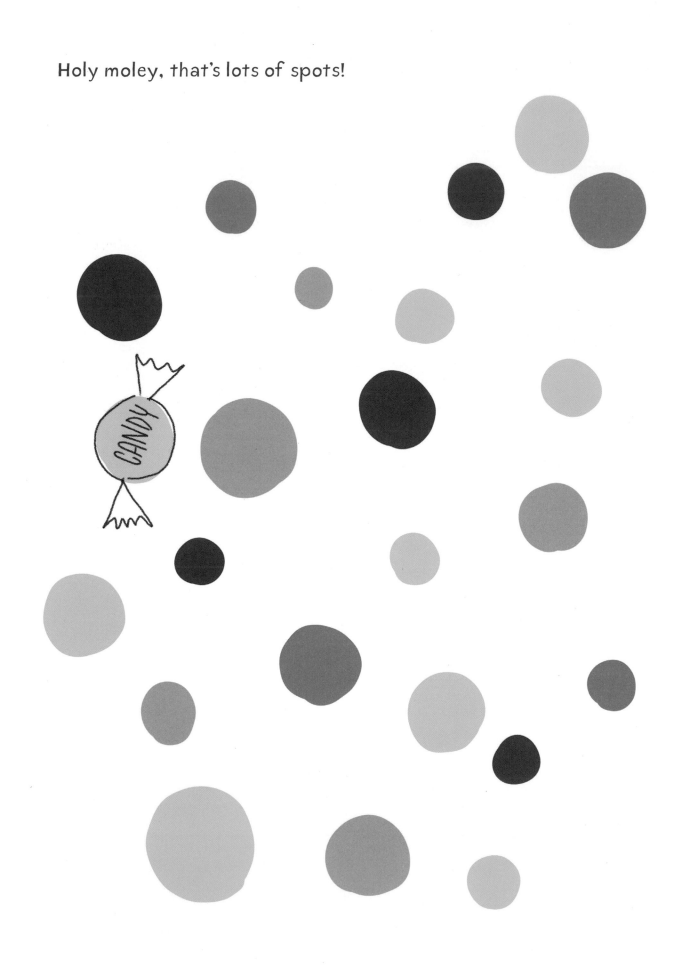

Use your imagination and
doodle your own pictures.

A cyclops has only one eye.
What do you imagine it looks like?
What kind of clothes does it wear?

Hocus pocus! You're looking into a witch's cauldron that's spilling over. What is boiling in that goop? Could it be snakes, spiders, or snails? Doodle them inside.

How many frogs are sitting on that log?
Draw the rest of the log and the frogs sitting on top!

Looks like one jumped onto a lily pad. Ribbit!

Watch the hot-air balloons glide across the sky!
Doodle designs on all the balloons.

Add baskets hanging from the bottom of the balloons.
Draw people inside the baskets.

It's a pair of llamas looking at you!
Are they wearing glasses and bow ties?
Draw them around the eyes shown here.

Bath time! Draw who is in the bubble bath.
Is that a muddy pig or a smelly dog?

An alien asks you where you live.
Can you draw a map of how to get to Earth?
Put an X to show where you live.

If you could create your own planet,
what would it look like? Draw it here.

Create your own emojis! Draw happy, sad, silly, and mad faces. Do some emojis have cat ears and whiskers or horns and teeth?

Congratulations! You have completed this book and come full circle. Continue to use your imagination and draw art using the circles you see in the world around you.